Introdu

Prayer has t
hard and ea
have to be o... ...intelligence or possess any special
abilities to engage in prayer. It is open to the "little"
and the "least". It is the language of the dependent
and the desperate. And that includes all of us, if we
are looking at our lives honestly.

But it is hard (as anyone who has tried to grow in
this privilege and discipline knows well) because it
is a spiritual activity that runs counter to the sinful
desires and the self-trust that plagues each one of
us. Our will is unnaturally bent inward and needs
special grace from God to bend upward to Him.

Over the years - often in "the greenhouse of
prayer" (see life lesson #7); meditating on a truth of
Scripture; reading an edifying book; slowly putting
the pieces together during a difficult season of
life; and sometimes thinking through a helpful
conversation with a friend (or foe) - I have been
given an insight into prayer that has helped me to
move a little farther in this joyful, yet often difficult
journey.

My prayer is that what has taken me decades to
learn, you will be able to learn and put into practice
in a much shorter time, and that God will equip
more people to become people of prayer in this
generation... for this generation.

Tim Kerr, August 2019

CONTENTS

01

THE HARDEST THING ABOUT PRAYER

The hardest thing about prayer is the small gap between thinking about praying and actually praying—that is, JUST TO BEGIN. The will to START praying requires supernatural help, or the deceitfulness of sin will delay the impulse to "later" (when I'm more rested; when I have more time; when I'm not feeling so stressed; etc.).

Is my main mode of prayer delay? Or do I actually pray when prompted to pray?

02

HOW TO GET A PASS TO THE PALACE

No one walks into the Oval Office at will for a chat with the president. You have to be summoned. You have to be vetted. Access to people in high places is impossible without access being granted.

So how do sinners (even justified sinners) get access to a holy God who lives in high places?

> I will make him draw near, and he shall approach me, for who would dare of himself to approach me? declares the LORD.
>
> *Jeremiah 30:21*

Our high priest brings the necessary sacrifice to gain access to God and, astonishingly, it is Himself. This offering fully satisfies God's justice and eliminates every barrier between us and Him. He holds out His scepter to invite us into the Holy of Holies. Our access in prayer is not based on our own worth or sincerity, but on Christ, who represents us to God. **This is what it means to pray in Jesus' name.** We are granted access to places we could never get to without Him.

> For through him we both have access in one Spirit to the Father.
>
> *Ephesians 2:18*

The principle of access is beautifully illustrated by Esther's bold entrance into the king's inner court:

> All the king's servants and the people of the king's provinces know that if any man or woman goes to the king inside the inner court without being called, there is but one law—to be put to death, **except the one to whom the king holds out the golden scepter so that he may live.** But as for me, I have not been called to come in to the king these thirty days.
> *Esther 4:11*

> And when the king saw Queen Esther standing in the court, **she won favor in his sight, and he held out to Esther the golden scepter** that was in his hand. Then Esther approached and touched the tip of the scepter.
> *Esther 5:2*

> But only the high priest entered the inner room, and that only once a year, and **never without blood,** which he offered for himself and for the sins the people had committed in ignorance.
> *Hebrews 9:7*

> Therefore, brothers, since we have **confidence** to enter the Most Holy Place **by the blood of Jesus...** let us draw near to God.
> *Hebrews 10:19,22*

What am I trusting in for the acceptance of my prayers? Am I expressing that clearly in my prayers?

03

THE PARADOX OF PRAYER:
What comes first, the chicken or the egg?

We need to pray in order to pray. A little prayer leads to more prayer. A little neglect of prayer leads to much neglect of prayer. The negative habit of non-prayer is an extremely hard habit to kick but must always first be overcome before we can ever learn the positive habit of regular prayer.

Our first request in prayer must therefore be, "Lord, help me to pray!"

> Give us life, and we will call upon your name!
> *Psalms 80:18*

Have I gotten into the **habit** of "little" or "no-prayer"?

04

THE BIGGEST MISTAKE ROUTINELY MADE IN PRAYER

The biggest mistake routinely made in prayer is that we become aware of a need in our lives (or others') and we pray about the need. At first glance, this pattern of prayer seems to have nothing wrong with it. It is much harder to notice a book that is missing from a bookshelf than a new book that has been added. What is missing in this prayer equation?

Think of driving with all-season tires in the Canadian winter—lots of sliding and not a lot of traction in the snow and ice. Winter tires, on the other hand, grip the road in significant ways. So how does one get real traction in prayer? We get traction when we remind God of His promises, and ask Him to do what He has promised He will do.

> This is the confidence that we have toward him, that if we ask anything according to his will he hears us.
>
> *1 John 5:14*

> If you abide in me, and my words abide in you, ask whatever you wish, and it will be done for you.
>
> *John 15:7*

Need + Request = Potential Answer

Need + **Promise** + Request = Probable Answer

> We are to pray in faith and faith has to do with God's promises. If therefore we don't understand what God has promised, we can't pray at all.
> *John Owen, Volume 4, The Work of the Holy Spirit in Prayer, p. 276 (my modernization)*

> What God has promised, all that He has promised, and nothing else, are we to pray for
> *John Owen, Volume 4, The Work of the Holy Spirit in Prayer, p. 275*

Do I regularly and systematically pair God's promises with my prayer requests?

05

THE GENIE IN THE LAMP

The basic view of prayer that the world holds to is that God is the supernatural one who exists to grant our requests, much like Aladdin's genie in the lamp. In this prayer scheme—we are the one in control and God exists to serve us.

This twisted way of relating to prayer is easy to descend into when our prayers are guided more by our own desires than by Scripture. An example of this is the conversation the captain has with Jonah during the massive storm at sea:

> The captain went down after him. "How can you sleep at a time like this?" he shouted. "Get up and pray to your god! Maybe he will pay attention to us and spare our lives."
> *Jonah 1:6*

At the other end of the spectrum, we have Mary, the mother of Jesus, facing the staggering truth that she is going to give birth to a son without a human Father. Her response is to submit her will to God in prayer:

> Mary said, "Behold, I am the servant of the Lord; let it be to me according to your word."
> *Luke 1:38*

She powerfully demonstrates that we are the servant in the relationship, not God. It is His will, not ours, that we must pray to be accomplished.

> Your kingdom come, **your** will be done, on earth as it is in heaven.
> *Matthew 6:10*

Whose will drives my prayers?

06

THE RICE PRAYER

In most countries of the world people eat rice every day, and sometimes every meal. What are the prayers in the Bible that we should consider praying every day (a "rice prayer")?

Ephesians 1-3 is like the doctrinal door frame that holds the door of practice that is found Eph 4-6. How does the apostle Paul attach these two sections together? And what is the hinge that he uses? Paul connects the great provisions of redemption (chapters 1-3) to the lifestyle of the redeemed (chapters 4-6) with the hinge of a prayer for power. We find the heart of this prayer in Eph 3:16-19.

Power to welcome Christ's presence in us

The word "dwell" in verse 17 means to live comfortably, the way one lives in a home that feels like "Home Sweet Home". It means getting rid of everything in our hearts that grieves the Spirit (Eph 4:30) and adding to our lives everything that pleases him ("sowing" to the Spirit - see Gal 6:8b).

Power to comprehend Christ's love for us

The basic idea of love is understandable to a child. But to truly believe and rely on God's love for us in Christ, a supernatural grace of illumination needs to be given to us. Those who keep themselves in the love of God are best able to love God in return and to love others around them.

Am I praying daily for the Holy Spirit's power to help me welcome Christ's presence & trust fully in His love? Could it be that the lack of growth in my life (and others') is because I have neglected this "rice prayer"?

07

THE GREENHOUSE EFFECT: THE PRINCIPLE

Prayer is not just something we do, it's also a mode of existence where God does something in us. Like a greenhouse, God grows good things in our hearts when we pray (solutions to problems; guidance; strength to fight battles; etc). We need to pray more because prayer is an atmosphere where the Holy Spirit works and transforms us.

This principle is illustrated by the example of Moses and Joshua meeting face-to-face with God in the Tent of Meeting:

> Thus the LORD used to speak to Moses face to face, as a man speaks to his friend. When Moses turned again into the camp, his assistant Joshua the son of Nun, a young man, would not depart from the tent.
>
> *Exodus 33:11*

Whenever Moses went in before the LORD to speak with him, he would remove the veil, until he came out. And when he came out and told the people of Israel what he was commanded, the people of Israel would see the face of Moses, that the skin of Moses' face was shining.

Exodus 34:34-35

Could it be that the lack of solutions in our lives is because we remain in the "winter of non-prayer" rather than entering into the life of the greenhouse?

08

THE GREENHOUSE EFFECT:
THE PRACTICE

Why did Paul always give thanks for people in his prayers? And why are so few of our prayers given to thanksgiving for believers? (We typically ask a lot, but thank only a little).

Paul's prayers seemed to facilitate a new way of looking at people; a way in which believers are seen in light of who they will one day be, rather than in light of who they presently are. We enter the greenhouse of prayer, and our perspective on others changes. Paul's vision of glorified humanity was clarified in prayer, and changed the way he thought about struggling believers:

> **I thank my God in all my remembrance of you,** always in every prayer of mine for you all making my prayer with joy, because of your partnership in the gospel from the first day until now. And I am sure of this, that **he who began a good work in you will bring it to completion at the day of Jesus Christ.**

Philippians 1:3-6

C.S. Lewis expresses this truth with his characteristic profundity in his book "The Weight of Glory":

> It may be possible for each to think too much of his own potential glory hereafter; it is hardly possible for him to think too often or too deeply

about that of his neighbor.

The load, or weight, or burden of my neighbor's glory should be laid daily on my back, a load so heavy that only humility can carry it, and the backs of the proud will be broken.

It is a serious thing to live in a society of possible gods and goddesses, to remember that the dullest and most uninteresting person you talk to may one day be a creature which, if you saw it now, you would be strongly tempted to worship, or else a horror and a corruption such as you now meet, if at all, only in a nightmare.

All day long we are, in some degree, helping each other to one or other of these destinations.

It is in the light of these overwhelming possibilities, it is with the awe and circumspection proper to them, that we should conduct all our dealings with one another, all friendships, all loves, all play, all politics.

There are no **ordinary** people.

You have never talked to a mere mortal.

Nations, cultures, arts, civilization—these are mortal, and their life is to ours as the life of a gnat.

But it is immortals whom we joke with, work with, marry, snub, and exploit—immortal horrors or everlasting splendors.

The Weight of Glory (HarperOne, 2001), pp. 45-46.

Do I regularly thank God for others in light of who they will one day be?

09

DUMP-TRUCK PRAYERS

Prayer is not just words. It is a God-ward action. It is easy to accumulate burdens throughout the day, and to gradually let our soul become weighed down by cares, frustrations, and temptations. Like a magnet hovering over a box of iron filings, we have all sorts of anxious clutter that attaches itself to our souls—much like the burrs that stick to our woolly coats after a walk in the woods. Unfortunately, while our souls gradually stagger under the growing burden of anxieties, we often fail to recognize and respond to our increasingly weighted and heavy steps.

Darkness can slowly envelope our spirit and we do nothing, like sitting ducks. Sometimes prayer simply needs to take the form of entrusting burdens to God. This kind of prayer is an action of the heart more than involving words of the heart. We cast off what has accumulated.

It takes special humility of heart to be regularly involved in this kind of casting of our cares. Simply put, the proud try to handle things themselves rather than entrusting their cares to God as indicated by 1 Peter 5:6-7:

And God will exalt you in due time, if you humble yourselves under his mighty hand by casting all your cares on him because he cares for you.

1 Peter 5:6-7 NET

You take me out of the net they have hidden for me, for you are my refuge. Into your hand I commit my spirit; you have redeemed me, O LORD, faithful God.

Psalms 31:4-5

As you accumulate cares, do you also cast them on God? What cares are you carrying now that you should be casting?

10
MY LIFE RIGHT NOW
IS AN ANSWERED PRAYER

The Heidelberg Catechism, explaining Providence concisely, states that: "All things, in fact, come to us not by chance but from his fatherly hand" and that "All creatures are so completely in his hand that without his will they can neither move nor be moved".

But how does this come about? **Romans 8** tells us that our life in the present moment is God answering the secret prayers of the Spirit, for God's will to be accomplished in our life:

> The Spirit himself intercedes for us with groanings too deep for words. And he who searches hearts knows what is the mind of the Spirit, because the Spirit intercedes for the saints according to the will of God.
> *Romans 8:26-27*

How is this prayer answered? It tells us in the next verse:

> And we know that for those who love God **all things work together for good,** for those who are called according to his purpose.
> *Romans 8:28*

These two verses bring together two secret works of God. The secret work of the Holy Spirit's prayers **for us** in our hearts, and the secret work of God **for us** in our circumstances. All things in our life are working together for good; that is, the Spirit's prayer for God's will to be worked out in our lives is being answered in our circumstances.

"All things work together for good". What specifically is that good? Verse 29 tells us.

> For those whom he foreknew he also predestined **to be conformed to the image of his Son...**
>
> *Romans 8:29*

God's providence is working all things for your good—that is, not to make your life easy, but to mold you to resemble Jesus more and more.

This information, that can only be known via divine revelation, is intended to create both an **expectation,** and a **faith affirmation** in our hearts. The expectation is one of hope as we anticipate the future (vs 24-25), and the faith affirmation is the declaration of verse 31: **"God is for us!"** (compare Job 16:9 for an example of when this perspective is missing).

Have you affirmed in prayer that your present circumstances are an answer to prayer? Have you declared in prayer that God is **for you?**

11

DESIRE: THE DEATH...
AND LIFE OF PRAYER

Desire is both a problem and a solution for prayer.
It's a problem when impurity is allowed to reign
in our hearts. Nothing kills prayer faster than a
troubled conscience.

> Beloved, if our heart does not condemn us, we
> have confidence before God; and whatever we
> ask we receive from him, because we keep his
> commandments and do what pleases him.
> *1 John 3:21-22*

Confidence before God - that is, faith - is an essential
part of the prayer process. Uncleansed sin disturbs
the conscience and effectively kills prayer before it
can even begin.

> Now in a great house there are not only vessels
> of gold and silver but also of wood and clay,
> some for honorable use, some for dishonorable.
> Therefore, if anyone **cleanses himself from
> what is dishonorable,** he will be a vessel
> for honorable use, set apart as holy, useful to
> the master of the house, ready for every good
> work. So flee youthful passions and pursue
> righteousness, faith, love, and peace, along with
> **those who call on the Lord from a pure heart.**
> *2 Timothy 2:20-22*

On the other hand, desire also fuels prayer. No one grows in their prayer life without discipline, and the fuel for consistent discipline is strong godly desires. Someone who exercises regularly does so because they have a strong desire to be fit or to look good—without those desires the discipline wouldn't have staying power.

Prayer can't be sustained simply by the sense that we should do it. It needs to be propelled by strong desires (Ps 63:1). The story of the man disturbing his friend at midnight asking for bread illustrates this. He is granted his request because of his shameless persistence (Luke 11). That is strong desire that won't be denied!

A sense of desperation is the heart of prayer—prayer is sustained by strong desires for something beyond the status quo.

What does the present state of your prayer life reveal about the desires that are ruling in your heart?

12

PRAYER IN THE HOLY SPIRIT: Part 1

> Take... the sword of the Spirit, which is the word
> of God, praying at all times in the Spirit, with all
> prayer and supplication.
>
> *Ephesians 6:17-18*

In Eph 6, the command to pray in the Spirit follows
the command to be filled with the Spirit in Eph 5:18
and the prayer for the Spirit's power in Eph 3:16-19.

So what does it mean to pray "in the Spirit"
according to this context?

It seems to indicate that prayer in the Spirit is
something that helps us effectively use God's word
while praying. Prayer in the Spirit is Scripture-
saturated prayer.

Like Arthur in the Disney fable "The Sword in the
Stone", who alone could remove the sword Excalibur
from the stone that held it, so also only Spirit-
filled believers are able to harness the Scriptures
effectively when in spiritual battles. Jesus effectively
used Scripture in His battle with Satan in the
wilderness because He was filled with the Spirit:

Jesus, **full of the Holy Spirit,** returned from the Jordan and was **led by the Spirit** in the wilderness for forty days, being tempted by the devil. ...The devil said to him, "If you are the Son of God, command this stone to become bread." And Jesus answered him, **"It is written,** 'Man shall not live by bread alone.'"

Luke 4:1-2,4

When we pray, do we pray "in the Spirit"?

13

PRAYER IN THE HOLY SPIRIT: Part 2

Obedience to the Spirit and prayer in the Spirit go hand in hand. Can I be grieving the Spirit on the one hand but also be led by the Spirit into prayer? Not likely. When I am walking in the Spirit, it is like driving a moving car—the steering wheel moves easily to steer the car in new directions (See Luke 2:25-28). But when I am grieving or resisting the Spirit in my life it is like sitting in a car parked in the driveway. Moving the steering wheel is very difficult.

> Whatever we ask we receive from him,
> because we keep his commandments and do
> what pleases him.
> *1 John 3:22*

When I am living in the Spirit, the Spirit will easily move me to pray in the Spirit (to pray about people and topics as He prompts; to pray with added faith; to pray with added fervency; to persevere until the answer comes; etc.) To pray in the Spirit, then, is to pray when the Spirit moves in our hearts and helps us to desire and seek God's will. It is the Spirit imparting the heart of God to us in the moment. When we pray in the Spirit, as John Owen says so compellingly, "we see a sight of God as on a throne of grace" and we know He welcomes our prayers to Him.

If a sinner comes to God seated on the throne of judgement he will feel nothing but dread and terror and will foolishly try to avoid him and his displeasure... where men have 'a spirit of bondage to fear', they can never have any delight in approaching God. This is removed by the Spirit of grace and supplication which consists of two things: enlarged liberty in speaking to God in prayer, and confidence of being heard and accepted.

John Owen, The Spirit and the Church, p.111

Are my prayers the overflow of a certain kind of life lived before God? Or do I sputter out gasping prayers choked by a life of spiritual compromise?

14

THE POSTURE OF PRAYER:
My Life is a Prayer

> Prayer is like breathing... if you don't, you can't.
> *Harold Burchett, Wisdom Words*

What if prayer became a mode of existence—in the way we constantly think and talk to ourselves—except that God was brought into that inner dialogue? Thinking our thoughts about Him, with Him, about everything—but with God, not just ourselves. Bringing our fears, frustrations, doubts, anguish, boredom, plans etc. before him. Starting the day with Him in faith-filled anticipation, and finishing the day in gratitude for His faithfulness:

> ... To declare your steadfast love in the morning, and your faithfulness by night.
> *Psalms 92:2*

This can be done. It is the Spirit-filled life applied to prayer. Being moved by the Spirit to continually live with a faith-sense of living in the presence of God.

This is essential as Christians are increasingly marginalized and opposed. How should we respond to hatred and accusations? Prayer.

> In return for my love they act as my accusers;
> **But I am in prayer.**
> *Psalms 109:4 NASB*

The Hebrew of Ps 109:4 literally says, **"But I - prayer"**. The ESV renders the phrase, "I give myself to prayer". The NET Bible, "I continue to pray". The NIV, "I am a man of prayer".

> Be constant in prayer.
> *Romans 12:12*

> Pray (present imperative—pray habitually as a way of life) without ceasing.
> *1 Thessalonians 5:17*

> The seeking believer becomes vigilant by **"praying without ceasing"** which implies also constantly using "wordless prayers."
> *The Discovery Bible*

Do I live with a faith-sense of God's presence, so that my internal thoughts, and my conversations with others, are seamlessly turned into prayer throughout the day?

15

FAITH AFFIRMATIONS:
Extended Amens

Faith affirmations are expressed everywhere in
Scripture and are probably the least used aspect of
prayer for most believers—except at the end of their
prayers when they say "amen". But few use their
amens as true faith affirmations at the end of their
prayers—"let it be so Lord!", "I believe this", "It is so",
"This can be relied upon", "truly!". Instead amen is
simply used in most cases as people use a period
at the end of the sentence—it marks that you are
finished praying.

In Psalm 89:15 it speaks of a faith declaration that
goes together with those who live with a faith-sense
of God's presence:

> Blessed are the people who know **the festal
> shout,** who walk, O LORD, in the light of your
> face.
> *Psalms 89:15*

This is the same word that is used in Joshua 6:20:

> As soon as the people heard the sound of the
> trumpet, the people shouted **a great shout,** and
> the wall fell down flat, so that the people went
> up into the city, every man straight before him,
> and they captured the city.
> *Joshua 6:20*

What was this joyful shout? It was a declaration of trust in God in spite of the circumstances. It was the exact opposite of the unbelief shown in the face of other intimidating walls (Num 13:28,31).

Faith declarations are neither requests nor strictly words of praise. They are instead declarations about God and what He will do. They are verbal declarations of trust. They are expanded "amens" if you will. These faith declarations speak faith but also grow our faith when we use them. Here are a few examples:

> In peace I will both lie down and sleep; for you alone, O LORD, make me dwell in safety.
> *Psalms 4:8*

> I will not be afraid of many thousands of people who have set themselves against me all around.
> *Psalms 3:6*

> The LORD is my light and my salvation; whom shall I fear? The LORD is the stronghold of my life; of whom shall I be afraid?
> *Psalms 27:1*

> I have set the LORD always before me; because he is at my right hand, I shall not be shaken.
> *Psalms 16:8*

> When I am afraid, I put my trust in you.
> *Psalms 56:3*

Do I regularly express faith in my prayers using Scripture to do so?

16
HONESTY IN PRAYER

It is quite common to pray in a way that stifles, or fails to express, what we are truly thinking and feeling about an issue. Our Father sees it all anyway, so why would we try to hide our true feelings in prayer?

One of the ways to maintain proper respect toward God, and yet still speak with heart-felt honesty, is to ask questions in prayer. The Scripture gives us many examples of this:

> Awake! Why are you sleeping, O Lord?
> Rouse yourself! Do not reject us forever!
> *Psalms 44:23*

> Why, O LORD, do you stand far away? Why do you hide yourself in times of trouble?
> *Psalms 10:1*

> How long must your servant endure? When will you judge those who persecute me?
> *Psalms 119:84*

> I will ponder the way that is blameless. Oh when will you come to me?
> *Psalms 101:2*

My God, my God, why have you forsaken me? Why are you so far from saving me, so far from the words of my groaning?

Psalms 22:1

O LORD, why do you cast my soul away? Why do you hide your face from me?

Psalms 88:14

Righteous are you, O LORD, when I complain to you; yet I would plead my case before you. Why does the way of the wicked prosper? Why do all who are treacherous thrive?

Jeremiah 12:1

Have my prayers truly expressed how I am feeling? Or are they "manufactured piety" that makes me a hypocrite each time I pray?

17

TRUE COMMUNION IS USUALLY EXPERIENCED IN THE UN-IDEAL

Rarely does the present moment feel ideal for communion with God. We are tired. We have work to do. We are feeling discouraged. Or afraid. Or angry. Or maybe we are just bored. The kids require my attention. My health is not so good. I'm stressed. I've got other commitments that I can't leave undone. Or maybe I just don't feel like it. Seeking God's face and living in the light of His presence never seems convenient in the moment. "Later maybe...".

The illusion is in thinking that we can put this off until we are uninterrupted by pressing schedules and deadlines. Perhaps during a holiday. But holidays are often the hardest time of all to break away from the routine to pray and seek God's face.

The truth of the matter is that some of the most exalted passages in Scripture on drawing near to God are written in the middle of un-ideal circumstances.

Consider the following:

> One thing have I asked of the LORD, that will I seek after: that I may dwell in the house of the LORD all the days of my life, to gaze upon the beauty of the LORD and to inquire in his temple.
>
> *Psalms 27:4*

This request is written when the Psalmist is surrounded by enemies on all sides who are trying to kill him!

> Nevertheless, I am continually with you; you hold my right hand. You guide me with your counsel,and afterward you will receive me to glory. Whom have I in heaven but you? And there is nothing on earth that I desire besides you. My flesh and my heart may fail,but God is the strength of my heart and my portion forever.
>
> *Psalms 73:23-26*

This "confession of faith" is uttered in the midst of deep doubts and disillusionment about the unfairness of life.

> Then I will go to the altar of God, to God my exceeding joy, and I will praise you with the lyre, O God, my God.
>
> *Psalms 43:4*

This is uttered by the Psalmist during a time of deep discouragement and feeling forgotten by God.

Am I waiting for ideal circumstances to truly seek God and commune with Him? Or am I able to commune with Him in the stress and messiness of my daily un-ideal life?

18

ACCEPTING GOD'S WILL THROUGH PRAYER (C.U.E.)

This is not to be confused with fatalism or irresponsible passivity. Rather, this heart action is essential when we do not **C**ontrol, **U**nderstand, or **E**njoy our circumstances. In fact, it is essential in all circumstances, but especially so when life becomes difficult.

> Pray without ceasing, give thanks in all circumstances; for this is the will of God in Christ Jesus for you.
> *1 Thessalonians 5:17-18*

I have found it helpful to think of this using a two-circle illustration. The first circle (the smaller of the two) is found within the larger circle. The small circle represents what God has entrusted to our control. We might label this smaller circle "self-control". We control what we wear, what we think, what we say, how we drive, how much we eat, etc. It might not be easy to exercise self control in these areas, but it is possible none-the-less.

But the larger circle is another matter entirely. This circle represents everything in our life that we don't control. In this circle we could put the weather, world events, the future, difficult trials that "drop" into our lives, what other people think, our innate intelligence, the degree of "success" that God entrusts to us, the limits of our abilities and gifts, etc.

What is to be done in such cases? We can complain and resist and get discouraged by our lot in life, or we can cheerfully, with peace in our heart, submit ourselves fully to God's perfect plan. Whether prosperity or poverty, success or failure, popularity or obscurity, health or sickness, at the top of the mountain or at the bottom of the valley, whatever God has assigned to us, we choose to embrace—willingly and cheerfully, in submission and surrender to His sovereign plan.

As the Heidelberg Catechism states so eloquently, "All things in fact, come to us not by chance but from his fatherly hand."

> Only let each person lead the life that the Lord has assigned to him, and to which God has called him. This is my rule in all the churches.
> *1 Corinthians 7:17*

This is really just another way of talking about God's Providence and our godly response to it. We not only acknowledge that God is in control of all things at all times, but we freely submit to His will even though the assignment may be very difficult.

> Whatever my lot, thou hast taught me to say,
> "it is well, it is well with my soul"
> *Horatio G. Spafford, It Is Well with My Soul, 1873*

What do you understand by the providence of God?

Providence is the almighty and ever present power of God by which he upholds, as with his hand, heaven and earth and all creatures, and so rules them that leaf and blade, rain and drought, fruitful and lean years, food and drink, health and sickness, prosperity and poverty—all things, in fact, come to us not by chance but from his fatherly hand.

How does the knowledge of God's creation and providence help us?

We can be patient when things go against us, thankful when things go well, and for the future we can have good confidence in our faithful God and Father that nothing will separate us from his love. All creatures are so completely in his hand that without his will they can neither move nor be moved.

Heidelberg Catechism, 1563,
taken from Take Words With You, 2015, p. 21-24

My Father, if it be possible, let this cup pass from me; nevertheless, not as I will, but as you will.
Matthew 26:39

My Father, if this cannot pass unless I drink it, your will be done.
Matthew 26:42

Now is my soul troubled. And what shall I say? 'Father, save me from this hour'? But for this purpose I have come to this hour. Father, glorify your name.
John 12:27-28

I trust in you, O LORD; I say, "You are my God." My times are in your hand.
Psalms 31:15

Have I learned to say in my prayers, "Not my will but yours be done?"

19

THE SONG OF THE HEART SET FREE

A beautiful metaphor for the Spirit-filled life is "a song". Note the contrast between the man under the control of sin and the one under the control of God's Spirit:

> An evil man is ensnared in his transgression, but a righteous man sings and rejoices.
> *Proverbs 29:6*

> **Be filled with the Holy Spirit, singing** psalms and hymns and spiritual songs among yourselves, and making music to the Lord in your hearts.
> *Ephesians 5:18-19*

> By day the LORD commands his steadfast love, and at night **his song is with me, a prayer** to the God of my life.
> *Psalms 42:8*

> The LORD is my strength and my song; he has become my salvation.
> *Psalms 118:14*

Is there a song in my heart when I pray? If not, why not?

20
HUMILITY BREEDS PRAYER

If my people who are called by my name **humble themselves, and pray and seek my face** and turn from their wicked ways, then I will hear from heaven and will forgive their sin and heal their land.

2 Chronicles 7:14

And when he was in distress, he entreated the favor of the LORD his God and **humbled himself greatly before the God of his fathers. He prayed to him,** and God was moved by his entreaty and heard his plea and brought him again to Jerusalem into his kingdom. Then Manasseh knew that the LORD was God.

2 Chronicles 33:12-13

Seek the LORD, all you humble of the land, who do his just commands; seek righteousness; **seek humility...**

Zephaniah 2:3

In the pride of his face the wicked does not seek him.

Psalms 10:4

Could it be that my lack of prayer is primarily a pride issue?

21

PRAYER INVOLVES LISTENING NOT JUST TALKING

God speaks, guards, and guides us through His word and Spirit. Isa 50:4 is a Messianic passage about Christ (see vs 6 etc.). It gives us significant clues into Jesus' prayer life and how He operated in prayer:

> The Lord GOD has given me the tongue of those who are taught, that I may know how to sustain with a word him who is weary. Morning by morning he awakens; **he awakens my ear to hear** as those who are taught.
> *Isaiah 50:4*

> I do nothing on my own authority, but speak just as the Father taught me.
> *John 8:28*

> When you walk, they will **lead you;** when you lie down, they will **watch over you;** and when you awake, they will **talk with you.**
> *Proverbs 6:22*

> The Spirit said to Philip, "Go over and join this chariot."
> *Acts 8:29*

Do I listen when I pray—or just talk?

22

LOVE HER OR HE WON'T LISTEN

Many times the blockage to answered prayer lies in a corner easily neglected and overlooked. When Jesus tells us to love our neighbour, the closest neighbour to us, when we are married, is our spouse. When I fail to show respect to my wife or listen to her with empathy, my prayers get blocked. Love opens the door to prayer, just as loveless living closes it.

> Husbands, live with your wives in an understanding way, showing honor to the woman as the weaker vessel, since they are heirs with you of the grace of life, **so that your prayers may not be hindered.**
> *1 Peter 3:7*

Could it be that my prayers remain unanswered because of a lack of love toward my spouse?

Made in the USA
Columbia, SC
12 February 2020

87729464R00028